Yesterday's Written Butterflies

Nery Joy Ochea

Ukiyoto Publishing

All global publishing rights are held by

Ukiyoto Publishing

Published in 2024

Content Copyright © Nery Joy Ochea

ISBN 9789362699503

All rights reserved.
No part of this publication may be reproduced, transmitted, or stored in a retrieval system, in any form by any means, electronic, mechanical, photocopying, recording or otherwise, without the prior permission of the publisher.

The moral rights of the author have been asserted.

This is a work of fiction. Names, characters, businesses, places, events, locales, and incidents are either the products of the author's imagination or used in a fictitious manner. Any resemblance to actual persons, living or dead, or actual events is purely coincidental.

This book is sold subject to the condition that it shall not by way of trade or otherwise, be lent, resold, hired out or otherwise circulated, without the publisher's prior consent, in any form of binding or cover other than that in which it is published.

www.ukiyoto.com

Dedication

For myself, the OCHEA family, and the special person in my heart, Gideon Louie Visbal

Contents

Day One – Echoes Within	1
Day Two - Reverie	3
Day Three - Resurgence	4
Day Four - Sunset	5
Day Five – Dancing Light in the Rain	6
Day Six – The Words of Her Cries	8
Day Seven - Memories	9
Day Eight – Sparks of Yesterday's Mourns	11
Day Nine – Stardust and Rains	13
Day Ten – Tonight's Tomorrow	15
Day Eleven – It's Okay	17
Day Twelve = Yesterday is Tomorrow	18
Day Thirteen – I'm Home	19
Day Fourteen – Where Do I start, I wonder?	20
Day Fifteen – Sorrowful Solitude	21
Day Sixteen – I'm Lost	22
Day Seventeen - Pen	23
Day Eighteen – Silent Loud Weeps	24
Day Nineteen – Butterfly Under the Moonlight Glimpse	25
Day Twenty – Heart Felt	28
Day Twenty-One – Wisdom's Streams	30
Day Twenty-Two - Escape	32
Day Twenty-Three – Dots of Thoughts	33

Day Twenty-Four – Lost in the Meantime	34
Day Twenty-Five - Trust	35
Day Twenty-Six – Shadows Within Reach	37
Day Twenty-Seven – Do I Still Breathe?	38
Day Twenty-Eight - Dream	40
Day Twenty-Nine – Blinded Reality	41
Day Thirty – Broken Glass	42
Day Thirty One - Doubt	43
About the Author	*44*

Day One
Echoes Within

If the mountains of the south and west did not collide,

I wonder if you'd plant the promises in the northern hemisphere?

What could be life like if you chose to cross the ocean of the last sparks in the daylight? Would there be any way for our bridge to hold in the middle of the lonely heart?

The wind whistling through the meadows of the colored auroras,

What a beautiful sight—

A lonely memory for us.

We used to hold the hand of the stars,

Now, breaking through zillion meteor showers.

The broad daylight is my warm midnight,

Two worlds of different hemispheres, bridging on the south wing.

If the mountains of the south and west did not collide,

Will there be love, I wonder?

Your sweet 'my love' call through the bird's song,

Such a thrilling chase in every beat of the heart.

The colors of the wind's embrace,

Tickling the north western—catch my breath.

Water down the dry roads of New York City.

Wiggling in the dust of snow were the burning buried emotions,

Will you ever come back to re-live the dying soul,

Or you'll just find the meadows of your great passion.

Regrets crossed the sea of grief,

What makes it brewing in the cold breeze.

Teach me not to drown,

Come and color the skies of regrets.

Day Two
Reverie

Tiptoeing on the mountain stream,

Dancing on the lodge of the lost dream.

Humming through the breath of sparks,

Mending the little stitches of the morning hearts.

The bottom of the spine wiggled in the air,

He or she or they might baffle the long-lost lair.

They seek no harm; all they want is to spread love,

Through the forest, where dances can echo above.

Mumbling—the mouth went on,

Whispering the colors of the meadows through evening sorrows.

"Kiss it," with symphony the voice commanded,

And so, she—voila! The sea hopped with joy.

Tiptoeing, tiptoeing, the toes went again.

On the lodge of the once's lost dream.

Now has spread the colors—rainbow sang,

The song of great triumph under the skies of struggles.

Day Three
Resurgence

Tomorrow, I'm going to fly through the tears of euphoria, Breathing away the struggles of yesterday y's torment.

My fingers twindled across the beautiful greed,

Pleasing anxiety with fear of twitch.

Tomorrow, I'm gonna smile—

Light of fortitude would beckon my soul.

Hora! I'm gonna be okay,

No matter where the wind takes me,

I will beat the agony of yesterday!

Day Four
Sunset

The kiss within the drop of love,

Shadowed the morrow's with ease.

Obfuscated reasons behind,

Suddenly becomes crystal clear—

There's a spark between the hearts of us.

Running through the veins of our fingertips,

The struggles we take in every little steps.

We face the future with great compassion and faith,

Making sure the bridge we tiptoed on,

Would never let us fall and break.

Holding on to the words your mouth formed,

During the sunset by the sea.

The warm kiss under the resting sun,

Woke up the tears with glee.

Between you and me, my love,

May the hands of our turns twindle—

With the slow music inside our chest,

Color the wheel with rainbow colors

Day Five
Dancing Light in the Rain

Droplets bathed the whole city,

Stopping feet on by the bus depo.

What a beauty of people,

Silently sharing serenity of the rain's orchestra.

Before their unread emotions,

Hides different thoughts that let time vanish for a while.

Afar from the distance,

A light touched the rain.

However, she felt unseen—

Unable to hold the droplets on its little hands.

It's painless, yet the thought was quite sour for her,

Sadness splashed on its face—she giggled.

The orchestra of the rain,

Held no tears on her eyes.

Such a beautiful nightmare,

She has to dance in the rain.

Trapping million memories on the surface of her journey.

What a life the light has!

Surely, unclear thoughts had been washed away.

Day Six
The Words of Her Cries

The bridge broke the broken ridge,
And the ridge was broken by the breaking bridge.
The promise listed with a kiss,
Has now kissed the promise with a laughing face.
Tickle, wiggle, waggle, walk—
Tiptoe, tiptoe, finger on the hook.
Giggle, wiggle, waggle walk—
The writer is crying on the corner of the book.

Day Seven
Memories

It seemed like it was just yesterday when we saw each other,

Together we shared memories and good laughter.

It seemed like it was just yesterday when you said, "I love you."

In the middle of our cries, I responded my feelings to you.

You hold my little hands when I am scared,

Looked at me with love and assured you're always there.

My heart leaps with great joy whenever I see your eyes.

I know I can trust you—no lies.

Walked through the shadows of dawn,

You made me laugh so I would not break.

I know it was the last minute,

But still you made it last for a bit.

Until the day you held your breath just to smile at me,

Before you see heavens, you assured I'm okay.

But how would I if you'll be no longer by my side?
I wish to be with you—but I can't.
Nay, the sky above is beautiful—painted in blue.
It has the same color as what I feel right now.
Sometimes I wonder if it is you,
The one who painted the sky to show me 'I miss you'.

Day Eight
Sparks of Yesterday's Mourns

Ticking under the bridge of laughter,

The hearts that beat for one another.

Warm souls wrapped together,

Painting the canvas of tomorrow's flower.

Beneath the smiling moon,

The eyes of worth thousand keepers laid evening kiss,

That borrowed the cold vines of hiss.

Up in the heavens, burst the colors of delight,

In my eyes, your beauty sparkled bright.

Oh, the fireworks of destiny overjoyed above,

The melody of hope and inspiration played within—love.

The tone of pace on each other's tail,

Footprints on the sand, the wisdom of the trail.

Holding your hand to the thousand stars in the galaxy,

Thawing the frozen gates of fallacy.

The liquid crystal running on your cheeks,

Showed the significance of leaving glitch.

Shadows of the future's journey fired through your blue eyes, In you, the truth folds; no spot of lies.

Woe! The literary arts wrote the voice of our story,

Forming the face of creative souls, poetry.

Surging in every letter that inked serenity,

Waving farewell to obscenity.

Yet bridges never last forever when the skies keep crying, No matter how hard I try to keep holding,

There's always a reason why I have to let go of the string. Into the pit of yesterday, I kept falling.

Alone in the dark, I'm weeping,

Your name escaped from my mouth, searching.

However, you were never found again.

Hura! Please don't let the night come to its end,

Bridges of memories will fade—broken!

The needles and threads would again try to mend,

The stitches of lilies on yesterday's garden.

Day Nine
Stardust and Rains

Feet tapping the road of great reflection,

Towering the rainbow of perfection.

Summoning beneath the soul of desperation,

The mother, clapping together with inspiration.

Hearts crying under the ocean of joy,

Wavering in the path towards light, turmoil.

Swords of the morrow's reminiscence stabbed the stone,

Laughter in the stars formed alone.

Carry the million stars with your hands,

On your own two feet, put the racket on and stand.

Up in the sky, cry with your might and laugh without doubt,

You're purely the diamond of yourself—shout!

You brought stardust unto the skies,

Clean your hands; color down the numbers of lies.

Footprints towards the stairs await your feet,

Step more and more until you make it to the 10th, at least.

Don't stop; keep going—you're doing great.

Tears may brush the trees of strings,
Don't be a loser, and keep moving.

Day Ten
Tonight's Tomorrow

Blended in the brush of fear,

Longing for trust alongside tomorrow's glimpse.

Pulling the rope of his guardian,

Beckoning the sparkles of the sun's rays.

Pour down the coffee of dust,

Under the moonlight dances the mourning love.

Music of the symphony played along,

Yet the crystal liquid in her eyes tells the story of longing.

Pick the shells of the night—

Whispering in the shores, the kiss within.

Hold the journey that rained through,

Dive into the thoughts of the morrow's story.

Pardon, borrow the hands of the art,

Paint on the canvas the twinkling stars.

Hold close to your heart the memoir of old agony,

Sweep the rhyming tease, folding presage afar.

Embrace the mark of the dream,

Lit up the fire of doubt—kill it.

Surrender the tears of depression; let laughter shine within your soul.

Don't forfeit the mountainous hindrances,

Your weapons to survive rest in your heart and mind.

Day Eleven
It's Okay

It's okay, no need to rush,

You'll be there in no time—hush!

Everything will be alright,

Don't make things tight.

Smile there, smile here,

And let your journey be guided with a light.

It's okay if you want to cry alone,

Not everyone can understand your pain after all.

It's not like you're weak because you can't tell them what's wrong, It's about making yourself a little strong.

It's okay if you're like a brittle twig,

Breaks when stepped on—defenseless.

There is no need to tell you're a pathetic pig,

Because not everyone can understand a life that you own.

It's okay, just be yourself and you'll be good.

It's okay, just smile to put you in the mood.

It's okay, don't rush, you'll make it there.

Believe in yourself, don't live in despair.

Day Twelve
Yesterday is Tomorrow

The world may not be as friendly as it seems,

But there is always a hidden gleam.

Not all people can understand what you feel,

But some others can drive with your wheel.

It doesn't matter if your friends are just three or two,

The important thing is that you value them, and so are you.

A circle of friends does not have to be a lot of numbers,

As long as they have ears for you, that's what matters.

Yesterday is tomorrow, I tell you, my friend.

What you shaped from the past will remain at the end

It's not about sticking your nose on the tip of the plate—

It's about learning to embrace your future that somehow looked bleak.

Don't hesitate to color the dark skies up in heavens,

You have the pencil, the painting, and everything.

It's you who hold the rules against your own fear,

Face it with or without the help of the one who's near.

Day Thirteen
I'm Home

It felt like yesterday since you crafted your imagination,

It seemed like it was quite far to form me into who I am today.

The inks of loneliness created a good masterpiece,

Showering the thoughts of both pain and happiness.

I witnessed your tears as you hold your pen unto me,

Inks following the lines of emotions.

Devouring your world into a book of your dream—

You brought me to life in a spink of eye.

Now, you hold me in your arms,

Your tears in a million sorrows suddenly melted.

Holding your dream in your hand is me,

Finally, I'm home, my author.

Day Fourteen
Where Do I start, I wonder?

Where do I start after crossing the next lane?

I wonder if there would be another to follow in this pane.

Where do I start after driving for miles and miles away,

I wonder if there is someone who would tell me today.

My friend, my friend,

Do listen to my little advice.

Do not let your shoulder be the crying lies.

Be the person to stand on your own no matter how lost you are,

For there are certain people who might drown you more.

Put the pot of courage on your stove,

Let it boil until it's ready to starve your hungry hopes.

Let your own way judge your mountains,

Into the wildest forest, you shine on your own star.

Day Fifteen
Sorrowful Solitude

Beating in the deep of the loner's chamber,
The color of the unseen tears.
Shed on the freedom of sworn lullabies,
The bittersweet memories she wants to erase.
Blackening in the mole's havoc,
The sword of hope pierced on the lilies.
Tomorrow shall lay down her lonestic fragrance,
Breathing beneath the dead heart—cold love.
Souring in her soul the mourns of wishes,
Her life, wasted in the darkening sorrows.

Day Sixteen
I'm Lost

I wish for the chains to unleash,

Free me without facing déath.

Hold my breath under the moonlight,

Silver tears screaming in the dark alley.

Unleash the weapon of tomorrow,

Let the future kiss the light—my fortune.

Let me hold the light of my life,

Unchain me from this prison.

Color the horses of missing feet,

Darkness lurking through my shadows.

Let me hold the breath—catch my soul!

Let me sleep unto great sorrow.

Day Seventeen
Pen

Bleeds on the clean paper,

A pen that holds one's breath.

Black ink crying out of the pen,

Curving letters with thousand shadows.

In the morning light,

Yesterday glows in the darkness.

The pen showered glorious gifts,

Changing the paper into such a beautiful piece of art.

Hold no close,

For the beauty will fade.

Tears of the pen,

Has not yet dried—broken.

Let the leg walk on its own,

Pacing the shadows of great resonance.

Visage on the sheet of paper,

Becomes the visage of the pen, which writes thousand colors.

Day Eighteen
Silent Loud Weeps

You see the thousand dirt on other people's eyes,
But you ignore yours.
You see the spotlight on other people's heads,
But you ignore yours.
You see the shadow of other people's bodies,
But you ignore what's yours.
Look in the mirror and see yourself,
Are you having a better smile than you think?
Look beneath your feet and observe,
Do you still walk the same as you do?
Look beneath your heart,
Are you still being you?

Day Nineteen
Butterfly Under the Moonlight Glimpse

Flew towards the glistening crystals,

Little embrace painted the smile of the little butterfly.

Beautiful soul dancing in the moonlight,

Tickled the butterfly's heart of glim.

Pecks of tease from behind,

Transpired the humming melody in the wind.

The legs carefully touched the crystal flowers,

Beckoning beneath, the loss of agony.

What a generous finger of dust,

Marking the empty canvas of the revengeful sea.

The yellow wings of the butterfly,

Mimicked the call of the night—

Kissed the shadow's rainbow by the mirror.

Into the stars, the butterfly's eyes colored,

Trimming the little ounces of chance to be anticipated. Shallow nets by the shore,

Listening to the whispers of the waves.

Will there be beauty in the sky by midnight,

They would sing great lullabies of the mermaid's songs. Butterfly by the moonlight,

Leapt to the woods of affection—

Trickling on its cheeks,

Tears of cheerful shadows.

Tickled in my feet, the success of yesterday's dream—
Become part of the literature's gleam.

Walked through the shadows,

Trust bridged on life's rainbows.

What a beautiful melody playing forward,

My heart danced and beat to its great tone.

Three stairs before me,

Beckoning my feet on the empty glass.

I wonder, I wonder,

Which of the three of them should I pass?

Looked closely on the morrow's clues.

Never had the chance—my sight on the loose.

Ah, success kissed the tip of my finger toes, I say.

But where do I start counting from that day?

What a beautiful start of the long run?

But comes to the end of the steep.

Looking for anything to grab me towards the next journey,

However, not a single eye looked at me.
Whistled, called the horses' alliance,
Silence brought me an empty list of guidance.
Carry me down the stream of shadows,
Hold my trophy up in the air—I'm bold.
Yet, where do streams lurk to find the escape—
Into the woods I strode, am I getting lost?
Questioned my own path,
Have the courage to break one's full triumph.
Hide no tears, I think I'm off the edge.
Further, should I seek or am I in the right place?

Day Twenty
Heart Felt

Both the lyrics and the melody of the song color the dance of the world, Not a single tone breaks the ear of the true audience.

Marking in one's eye,

The beat of heart—fall in love with her.

The tremble of the ocean wave clapped along the shores of laughter. Clinging beneath, the secret fantasy of sick reality.

Marching through the waters of a thousand horses,

The desire to take its breath away from the song.

Flowers of rain scattered with the wind's farewell,

Holding up haven, the future's bleak whispers.

The song has to fade;

Laughter and claps should remain.

Yet, what will be the symbol of true judgement if a fake reality masks its embrace? Hands of whirling hopes and gestures,

Comes across the methods of cheating desires.

Keeping both the spinning wheels on the shallow touch.

Can anyone pull the heavy shovel of the past?

Loads and loads and loads of unrealistic affection has made the pain more unbearable. Knife chained through their compliments,

Locked the door of great alliances.

Attempts to end the sorrow,

Colored the shifts of the forest—life.

Might sound sad and hopeless;

Yet thankful with heart felt.

The desire to live once more through the dark waves,

Leaned in one's thought for a while.

What could be the difference—

Nothing less could be seen.

Always seeking the truth,

An empty answer kiss within.

Live a little more, the song of the masked lonely poem would say, Crash through the broken glasses of dawn—

You'll find your way.

Because through the pains and shadows,

An empty soul can find its way to move forward,

With stronger colors vibrating in the moonlight

Day Twenty-One
Wisdom's Streams

The blanket of uncertainties waits for the sunrise,

The smell of tomorrow's wisdom colors the stream of hopes.

Footprints on the seashore would fade,

Yet the hearts that yearn for memories will never disappear.

Your words touched every meadow of extreme,

Your laugh giggled the thousand sadness.

Your stand before the others brought us the feeling of glee,

Your heart made us feel the soft version of ourselves.

You shaped us with beauty,

You colored us with confidence,

You flowered our gardens,

You throw us into the stage of success.

Tomorrow shall come—

Another will be at your place.

Yet it doesn't matter,

We can't have goodbyes at this moment.

March with a fire of wisdom within,

The people behind you will flame with courage and less pain.

Day Twenty-Two
Escape

The distance between the moon and the stars,
Kissing the loneliness of the heart.
Broken up through a million tears,
Learning to hover the wheel of yesterday.
Beckoning the feet of dust,
Whirling the truth off the edge of death.
Hop unto the door of fantasy,
Clean up the dirt of whiskey.
Wiggling in the middle of the night,
Embrace me—my darkest vein.
Sorrow laughing through the dark corner,
Teasing the light; shooing away its wings.

Day Twenty-Three
Dots of Thoughts

Through the ocean of great memories,
Swiming the roar of the future.
Healing the scars of yesterdays,
Here comes the cry of the fools.
Learning to walk on the water,
Fascinated by the power of one's faith.
There could be a reason behind—
Why some learn to fight on their own?
There might be some lurking spirit,
That's wandering and find themselves lost.
What could be the next hop of the journey?
I wonder what might be the rain's calling.
Water on the loose swam through heavens,
What does it mean? Storm.
The best failure that we have on the top,
Shall be the best lesson of the year.
Now, walk on the water with your hands,
And feel the faith within your heart.

Day Twenty-Four
Lost in the Meantime

My feet sauntered through the dark alley,

Beside the church of great sinners, I cried with golden tears. What have I done to myself that makes things heavy?

I don't find any answers, no matter how I try to find it.

Mothers of ascending dreams,

Where can I find the way to the next journey?

Will there be another chance for me to find the light?

Is there any way I can make it through?

And carry the beautiful sunrise in my back.

I'm lost in the meantime, I say.

My hands and feet are tied by the bay of hell.

Tomorrow, I should kiss the mourning shadows,

Yet my tears will have to break it free—forgive me.

Do I have to saunter in the middle of great execution?

Where do I find the word 'escape' in this destination?

I hope someone to hold my hand as I walk,

Because I know I will always be lost.

Day Twenty-Five
Trust

Tell yourself to put a bracket around,

Your heart may weaken from the dust—surrounded.

How do you brace the second chance,

If you knew you can't build the trust you once had.

Response in between rain and snow,

Look behind, do you see the upcoming sorrow?

Is before you the color of your shadow?

Or just the glimpse of the broken tomorrow.

Understand yourself and reflect love and kin,

Do you think change can color the rain?

What about the sunset within,

Does it make sense when you carry that yesterday pain?

Stand through your doubts,

Build a bracket beforehand.

No, it's not about being selfish—but are you?

Little did you know you're being a liar,

To yourself, and everywhere—not by far.

Take a turn—it's okay.

Clicking the keyboard of the same sound—ah, lavish!

Make it a bit clearer,

Do you still have trust in yourself and surrounded hell?

Day Twenty-Six
Shadows Within Reach

Holding up in one's thoughts,

The knot of communication.

Knocking through the shadows,

The voice of lurking creation.

What I see is what I don't understand,

I need someone to withstand—a lamp.

Bring the colors of clarification,

The true meaning of communication.

Shadows within reach,

I'm scared of the open sea.

Hold my tongue, dearest trust,

Pull the strength and glee.

Light up the road I once stopped crossing,

Bring my feet forward to the woods of greatness.

No, I do not seek yesterday,

But pure trust and happiness.

Day Twenty-Seven
Do I Still Breathe?

Where could be the air of time,
I couldn't find one in the dark.
Where is forgiveness?
I only see hate in the bark.
Is air waving goodbye?
Oh, I cannot breathe.
Does water still dance,
Please, help me escape.
In the middle of something in my life,
I don't know what's right and wrong.
In the middle of struggles in everyday eyes,
I could no longer feel pain—hush!
Tears may run down my cheeks,
But I feel so numb.
Everyone has left,
Brought with them my life—the lamp.
Do I still breathe in this unfair world?
I could no longer feel it, honestly.

Maybe tomorrow will crawl,
And have me smile with pain and glee.

Day Twenty-Eight
Dream

The color of the rainbow turned into something beautiful,

Something that I had always been dreaming of.

Depicted in the sunshine,

My loneliness of the past.

Dream of the mother who gave birth to sorrows,

Ah, the rainbow will color up the shadows.

Within every color,

Comes the meadows of effervescence.

Knitting the morrows' cry,

Held up in the arms of wet reality.

Make it stop—I feel lost in my dream.

"Hold the cup of tea in my fingernail, darlin',"

The voice of the gentle mother spoke.

No, I do not drink poison from the glamorous smile,

Pity, I can say—a dream that kills red blood.

Day Twenty-Nine
Blinded Reality

I always wanted to see the beauty of reality,
But I don't find the right window to peek on.
Where would I run to get out?
I hate living in nightmares of dreams.
People are struggling to get to know each other,
Quarreling, arguing, stabbing one another.
Babies cry on the shoulders of the youngsters,
Who are still eating their little fingers.
Ah, where do I escape from this nightmerous dream?
Where do I find the way to get out of the door.
This is something that I need to know—
Where can I see the true world?

Day Thirty
Broken Glass

Such a beautiful vase on the vanity,

Its colors wander around the room when the sun kisses it.

The water sparkles inside,

Blabbering the music of the heart.

Such beauty is fragile,

No one should hurt its feelings—

Do not dare to play with it,

Might fall to the ground and break.

Such beauty fell to its death—

Earthquake made it kiss its last breath.

Oh, what a pity to the beautiful vase,

Now it will never come back to its original shape.

Day Thirty One
Doubt

Lurking through the shadows of emptiness,
The words of longing answers.
Am I lost? Am I in the right place?
I could not find the right colors.
Hoping to get through the green leaves,
Dance with the wind of peace.
How will I ever know I'm in the right place?
When my tears keep falling down my cheeks.
I hold no trust within myself,
The words of wisdom are shaken.
What can I possibly do to walk on the mountains?
And never fly in the ground with broken wings

About the Author

Nery Joy Ochea

Nery Joy Ochea is a published author from Carigara, Leyte, Philippines. She currently owns 7 books published in in three different countries—Canada, Europe, and Philippines. Although not really known for her great passion in writing, Nery has always the spirit to keep the pen bleeding.

Most of her works are related to historical genres, psychological, tragic-romance, science and dystopian fiction. Her words are exceptional. She has this type of writing that needs a full understanding of the context, rather than just simply reading. She aims to capture the heart of people who are into books and literary and caress their hearts with her deep messages. She is not afraid to open the eyes of issues through her poems and novels— Nery always wants to keep the voices of the society be amplified in the future and find the way for them to keep living with purposes.

Currently, she is a dedicated Bachelor of Arts in Communication student at Biliran Province State University in Naval, Biliran. She aims to be one of the BA Comm students, who may hear the voice of the whimpering issues that could possibly be solved through the voice of literary.

www.ingramcontent.com/pod-product-compliance
Lightning Source LLC
LaVergne TN
LVHW041556070526
838199LV00046B/1999